What Matters Most
BARBRA STREISAND
SINGS THE LYRICS OF ALAN AND MARILYN BERGMAN

This book was approved by Barbra Streisand

Cover photo courtesy Studio Russell James

Piano/vocal arrangements by John Nicholas

Cherry Lane Music Company
Director of Publications/Project Editor: Mark Phillips

ISBN 978-1-60378-399-6

Visit our website at www.cherrylaneprint.com

From the Way We Were...
To the Way We Are....

Alan and Marilyn Bergman have a remarkable gift for expressing affairs of the heart. To give you some idea as to how much I admire their lyrics, I've already recorded 51 of their songs…and with this new collection it will be 63!

I met Alan and Marilyn when I was about 18 years old. They were young writers who had come to the attention of *Funny Girl* and *Gypsy* composer Jule Styne. He was set to produce a Broadway show they'd written with composer Sammy Fain titled *Something More!* After a long day of auditioning singers, Jule encouraged them to check out this new "kid" who was playing nightly at the Bon Soir. They came…we met…and that is essentially how our love affair began.

I started out as an actress. When I couldn't get work I began to sing as a way of supporting myself, but I always approached each song as an actress first. Many of Alan and Marilyn's songs are written for motion pictures, which is why their lyrics are so often character driven. Like a script, their writing gives the actress in me something to interpret. Many of their songs are like miniature three-act plays, which begin with a question and then resolve with a deeper understanding.

The subject they most often turn to is love, in all its guises. They truly understand the complex interaction of relationships—logical, illogical, challenging, passionate, sometimes disappointing, often enduring, but always interesting.

With so many love songs registered in the ASCAP catalog, one might ask, "How many more ways are there left to say 'I love you'?" Alan and Marilyn have found them. They have a great respect for the craft of songwriting and a fascination with both the meaning and texture of language. For someone who sings, their words and phrases always seem to land on the right notes… and that's by design not happenstance. Their lyrics have a poetic grace that's completely unique.

The most essential ingredient that makes Alan and Marilyn such consistently superb collaborators is that they are truly in love. Their spectacular marriage gives their lyrics an authenticity, making them both deeply personal, and at the same time, completely universal.

Of course, I couldn't sing their words if they weren't connected to such gorgeous melodies. Alan and Marilyn have always had impeccable taste when it comes to finding just the right collaborators—as you can tell by the composers whose songs are on this album—Jerry Goldsmith, Dave Grusin, Johnny Mandel, David Shire, John Williams, Lew Spence, and of course our long-time collaborator Michel Legrand.

The main reason I've made this album is that I want to thank Alan and Marilyn for a lifetime of love. Not only have they provided me with many beautiful songs to sing, but also as important, they've nurtured my soul and spirit. Ours has been a friendship of many shared passions about life, love, music and art…truth, justice, and beauty. We've crusaded for a multitude of social, political, and environmental causes together, because we deeply care about the state of the world. We've shared more delicious meals than I can remember…many cooked by Marilyn herself.

So to my dear Alan and Marilyn, I ask, "Can it really be decades since we first met?" It went by so fast…but I'm very happy that you and your magical words came into my life and equally happy you let me come into yours.

With Love,
Barbra Joan

New York 1983

What Matters Most...

To hear Barbra's voice in our minds, to imagine her singing what we write as we write always inspires us as we try to create something worthy of her great artistry.

She always gets exactly what we mean in a lyric. And more. The actor that she is, the director that she is, the singer that she is gets it. And more. Shadings, feelings, nuances emerge that never fail to surprise and thrill us.

How do you sing a question mark? A smile? How do you sing the text and subtext of a song while never sacrificing musicality for meaning or meaning for musicality? Never choosing style over substance or substance over style?

To hear Barbra sing a song we've written is to know why we chose to become writers.

She was 18 years old when we first saw her. Appearing at a club in New York's Greenwich Village. She stepped on the small stage in an outfit of her own creation: a full-sleeved white chiffon blouse, a vest and long skirt of menswear herringbone. An original. Everything about her was original. Then she sang "My Name Is Barbara" (a song of Leonard Bernstein's). The sound of her was unique. The beauty of her was unique. Everything was within her and before her.

We met backstage that first night. She had a tiny dressing room which she shared with Phyllis Diller (who was the headliner). One of us asked, "Do you know how wonderful you are?" She didn't answer, but she *had* to know. No one can be that wonderful and *not* know! That was over 50 years ago. We've never been out of each other's lives since then.

Two years ago the Academy of Motion Picture Arts and Sciences had an evening in tribute to us. Quincy Jones was the host. Many friends and colleagues took part in it. Michel Legrand came from Paris. Dave Grusin came from Santa Fe. John Williams from Boston, Marvin Hamlisch from New York, and Barbra.

Knowing how she dislikes appearing in front of a lot of people, we were all the more appreciative of her participation. And when she said, "My next album is going to be a tribute to you guys," we were speechless.

Not too long after, she began thinking about what songs she would include. She knew she wanted to do songs that she'd never sung before. She asked us to make a list for her consideration. Then her work of selecting, conceptualizing, singing began. Perhaps unconsciously, creating a dramatic context for herself for each song, as an actress would for a character or a scene.

With the brilliant orchestrator Bill Ross, the arrangement, the musical environment for each song was decided upon. Then came the most focused, careful work at her recording space which she calls "Grandma's House"—a small cottage on the grounds of her Malibu home. Rehearsing, discovering the songs.

We've been so blessed with wonderful melodies from great composers. Choosing between them couldn't be easy. Many were necessarily eliminated on the way to selecting the ten that would make the CD.

Finally, the day of the first session arrives. The eponymous Streisand Scoring Stage at Sony Studios is filled with Hollywood's finest musicians. The familiar sounds of setting up, tuning up, and chatter in anticipation of the first downbeat and Barbra's arrival. She walks into the studio and the air changes. Bill Ross steps onto the podium. The room quiets. There's excitement mixed with respect. It is always an event when Barbra Streisand sings— even for these musicians who have heard them all.

Marty and Jay, in the control room, smile and nod their appreciation. (A lyric writer or two have been known to cry!) She will make suggestions to Bill before the next take. They both know how to make it better. And that's what it's about, making it better. These are artists at the top of their game with the same goal: getting it as close to perfect as possible. And so it goes. She did four songs that first day. And five the next session, several weeks later.

On the way home in the car, she begins the next phase of her work—listening. She remembers every detail of every take. No detail is too small. Making it better…and better and better. Until she finally has to let it go.

How many times have we experienced that rare alchemy of words, music, Barbra? It's always as if it were the first time. And now this CD. How to put into words what we feel when we listen to it? Perhaps if there were a melody, we could find the words. It would certainly be a love song.

"Do you know how wonderful you are?"

It was just over 50 years ago that we met. Fifty years of working together, playing together, sharing holidays, birthdays, quiet times. Some sad, mostly happy. The world has changed around us, but our love for each other is a constant. Clearly, she is our muse. Sometimes daughter. Sometimes sister. Always beloved friend.

The three of us were born in the same Brooklyn hospital. Years apart. How fortunate we are to be alive at the same time.

Alan and Marilyn

CONTENTS

The Windmills of Your Mind

Theme from THE THOMAS CROWN AFFAIR

Words by
Alan and Marilyn Bergman

Music by
Michel Legrand

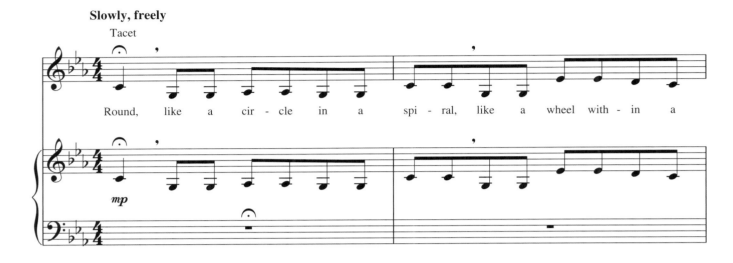

Round, like a cir-cle in a spi-ral, like a wheel with-in a

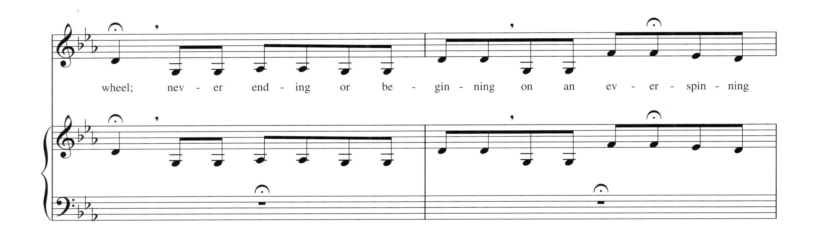

wheel; nev-er end-ing or be-gin-ning on an ev-er-spin-ning

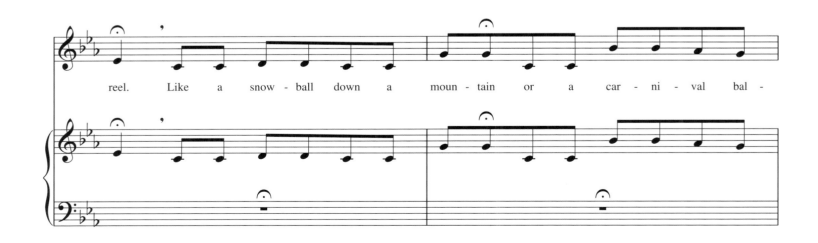

reel. Like a snow-ball down a moun-tain or a car-ni-val bal-

loon. Like a car - ou - sel that's turn - ing, run - ning rings a - round the

moon. Like a clock whose hands are sweep - ing past the min - utes of its

face. And the world is like an ap - ple whirl - ing si - lent - ly in

space; like the cir - cles that you find in the wind - mills of your

mind. Like a tun - nel that you fol - low to a tun - nel of its own; down a hol - low to a cav - ern where the sun has nev - er shone. Like a door that keeps re - volv - ing in a half - for - got - ten dream, or the rip - ples from a peb - ble some - one toss - es in a

10

song. Half - re - mem - bered names and fac - es, but to whom do they be -

long? When you knew that it was o - ver, you were sud - den - ly a -

ware that the au - tumn leaves were turn - ing to the col - or of his

hair. Like a cir - cle in a spi - ral, like a wheel ___ with - in a

wheel; nev - er end - ing or be - gin - ning on an ev - er - spin - ning

reel as the im - ag - es un - wind; like the cir - cles that you

find in the wind - mills of your mind.

Something New in My Life

from MIKI & MAUDE

Lyrics by
Alan Berman
and Marilyn Bergman

Music by
Michel Legrand

for you to come and fill the space in my heart

that long be - fore I said "I love you," I

loved _____ you. What - ev - er hap - pens, this is

true in my life, when all the springs have come and

Solitary Moon

Words and Music by
Alan Bergman, Marilyn Bergman
and Johnny Mandel

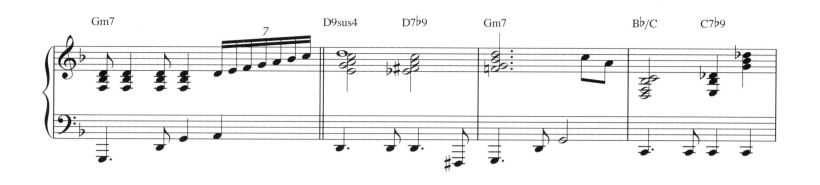

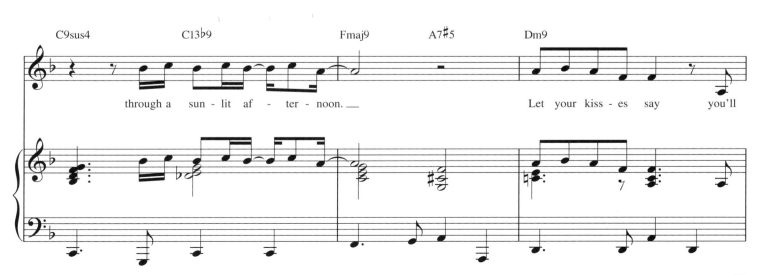

Nice 'n' Easy

Words and Music by
Lew Spence, Alan Bergman
and Marilyn Bergman

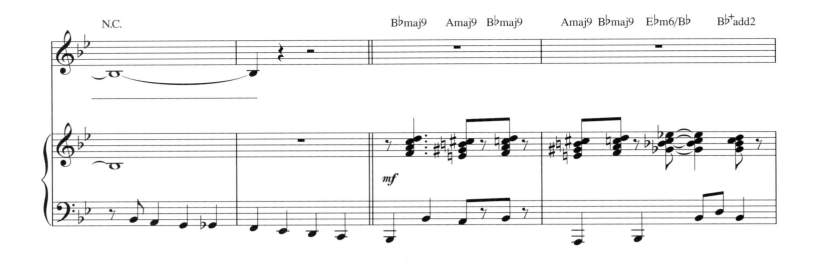

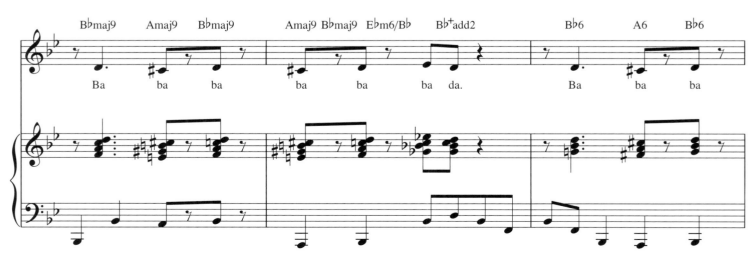

Alone in the World

Words and Music by
Alan Bergman, Marilyn Bergman
and Jerry Goldsmith

storm out there. You'll be _____ the on - ly

love that I've known in the world;

no clocks to meas - ure the time we

share. Out there the winds are bit - ter cold and there is

So Many Stars

Words and Music by
Alan Bergman, Marilyn Bergman
and Sergio Mendes

The Same Hello, the Same Goodbye

Lyrics by
Alan Bergman
and Marilyn Bergman

Music by
John Williams

empty feel - ings cou - pled with the won - d'ring why. What

words we said or left un - said, i - mag - in - ing what could have been or

should have been. But here we are; _____ we've come so far. Must

you and I say the same good - bye a - gain? _____

Tempo I

No fond fare - well, no sweet good - bye, just

emp - ty feel - ings cou - pled with the won - d'ring why. What

48

49

That Face

Words and Music by
Lew Spence
and Alan Bergman

I'll Never Say Goodbye

from the Universal Film THE PROMISE

Words and Music by
David Shire, Alan Bergman
and Marilyn Bergman

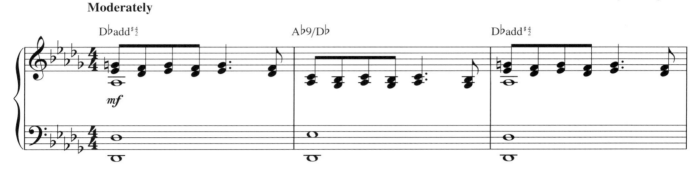

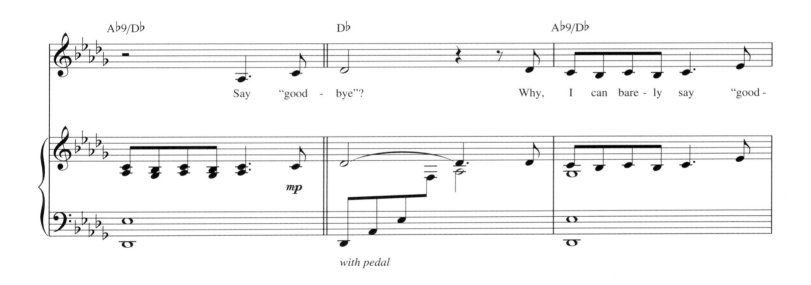

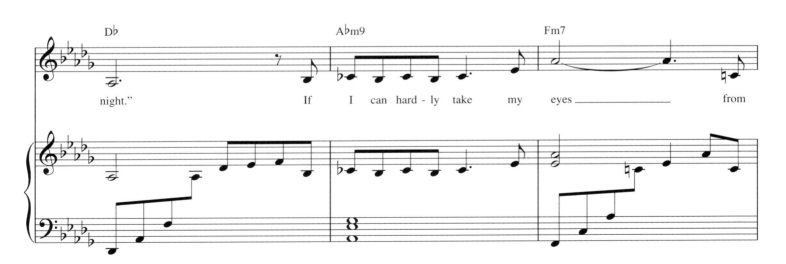

yours, how far can __ I go? _____ Walk a-

way? The thought would nev - er cross my mind. I

could - n't turn my back on spring or fall, your

smile _____ least of all. When __ I say

Tempo I

bye. We're danc-ers on a crowd-ed floor while

oth-er danc-ers live from song _____ to song. Our

mu - sic ___ goes on, on and on. _____ And

if I nev-er leave your arms, I real-ly will have trav-eled

What Matters Most

Lyrics by
Alan Bergman
and Marilyn Bergman

Music by
Dave Grusin

It's not how man-y sum-mer-times ___ we ___ had to give ___ to fall, the laugh - ter and the tears we grate-ful-ly ___ re - call; what mat-ters most is that we loved at all. ___

More Big-Note & Easy Piano Books

For a complete listing of Cherry Lane titles available, including contents listings, please visit our web site at www.cherrylaneprint.com

BEAUTIFUL POP BALLADS FOR EASY PIANO
31 lovely pop songs in simplified arrangements, including: Don't Know Why • From a Distance • Hero • Just Once • My Cherie Amour • November Rain • Open Arms • Time After Time • Unchained Melody • What a Wonderful World • Your Song • and more.
_____ 02502450 Easy Piano $12.99

CHOPIN FOR EASY PIANO
This special easy piano version features the composer's intricate melodies, harmonies and rhythms newly arranged so that virtually all pianists can experience the thrill of playing Chopin at the piano! Includes 20 favorites mazurkas, nocturnes, polonaises, preludes and waltzes.
_____ 02501483 Easy Piano $7.99

CLASSICAL CHRISTMAS
Easy solo arrangements of 30 wonderful holiday songs: Ave Maria • Dance of the Sugar Plum Fairy • Evening Prayer • Gesu Bambino • Hallelujah! • He Shall Feed His Flock • March of the Toys • O Come, All Ye Faithful • O Holy Night • Pastoral Symphony • Sheep May Safely Graze • Sinfonia • Waltz of the Flowers • and more.
_____ 02500112 Easy Piano Solo $9.95

BEST OF JOHN DENVER
A collection of 18 Denver classics, including: Leaving on a Jet Plane • Take Me Home, Country Roads • Rocky Mountain High • Follow Me • and more.
_____ 02505512 Easy Piano $9.95

JOHN DENVER ANTHOLOGY
Easy arrangements of 34 of the finest from this beloved artist. Includes: Annie's Song • Fly Away • Follow Me • Grandma's Feather Bed • Leaving on a Jet Plane • Perhaps Love • Rocky Mountain High • Sunshine on My Shoulders • Take Me Home, Country Roads • Thank God I'm a Country Boy • and many more.
_____ 02501366 Easy Piano $19.99

EASY BROADWAY SHOWSTOPPERS
Easy piano arrangements of 16 traditional and new Broadway standards, including: "Impossible Dream" from Man of La Mancha • "Unusual Way" from Nine • "This Is the Moment" from Jekyll & Hyde • many more.
_____ 02505517 Easy Piano $12.95

A FAMILY CHRISTMAS AROUND THE PIANO
25 songs for hours of family fun, including: Away in a Manger • Deck the Hall • The First Noel • God Rest Ye Merry, Gentlemen • Hark! the Herald Angels Sing • Jingle Bells • Jolly Old St. Nicholas • Joy to the World • O Little Town of Bethlehem • Silent Night, Holy Night • The Twelve Days of Christmas • and more.
_____ 02500398 Easy Piano $8.99

FAVORITE CELTIC SONGS FOR EASY PIANO
Easy arrangements of 40 Celtic classics, including: The Ash Grove • The Bluebells of Scotland • A Bunch of Thyme • Danny Boy • Finnegan's Wake • I'll Tell Me Ma • Loch Lomond • My Wild Irish Rose • The Rose of Tralee • and more!
_____ 02501306 Easy Piano $12.99

HOLY CHRISTMAS CAROLS COLORING BOOK
A terrific songbook with 7 sacred carols and lots of coloring pages for the young pianist. Songs include: Angels We Have Heard on High • The First Noel • Hark! The Herald Angels Sing • It Came upon a Midnight Clear • O Come All Ye Faithful • O Little Town of Bethlehem • Silent Night.
_____ 02500277 Five-Finger Piano $6.95

JEKYLL & HYDE – VOCAL SELECTIONS
Ten songs from the Wildhorn/Bricusse Broadway smash, arranged for big-note: In His Eyes • It's a Dangerous Game • Lost in the Darkness • A New Life • No One Knows Who I Am • Once Upon a Dream • Someone Like You • Sympathy, Tenderness • Take Me As I Am • This Is the Moment.
_____ 02500023 Big-Note Piano...................................... $9.95

JACK JOHNSON ANTHOLOGY
Easy arrangements of 27 of the best from this Hawaiian singer/songwriter, including: Better Together • Breakdown • Flake • Fortunate Fool • Good People • Sitting, Waiting, Wishing • Taylor • and more.
_____ 02501313 Easy Piano $19.99

JUST FOR KIDS – NOT! CHRISTMAS SONGS
This unique collection of 14 Christmas favorites is fun for the whole family! Kids can play the full-sounding big-note solos alone, or with their parents (or teachers) playing accompaniment for the thrill of four-hand piano! Includes: Deck the Halls • Jingle Bells • Silent Night • What Child Is This? • and more.
_____ 02505510 Big-Note Piano...................................... $8.95

JUST FOR KIDS – NOT! CLASSICS
Features big-note arrangements of classical masterpieces, plus optional accompaniment for adults. Songs: Air on the G String • Dance of the Sugar Plum Fairy • Für Elise • Jesu, Joy of Man's Desiring • Ode to Joy • Pomp and Circumstance • The Sorcerer's Apprentice • William Tell Overture • and more!
_____ 02505513 Classics.. $7.95
_____ 02500301 More Classics $8.95

JUST FOR KIDS – NOT! FUN SONGS
Fun favorites for kids everywhere in big-note arrangements for piano, including: Bingo • Eensy Weensy Spider • Farmer in the Dell • Jingle Bells • London Bridge • Pop Goes the Weasel • Puff the Magic Dragon • Skip to My Lou • Twinkle, Twinkle Little Star • and more!
_____ 02505523 Fun Songs.. $7.95

JUST FOR KIDS – NOT! TV THEMES & MOVIE SONGS
Entice the kids to the piano with this delightful collection of songs and themes from movies and TV. These big-note arrangements include themes from The Brady Bunch and The Addams Family, as well as Do-Re-Mi (The Sound of Music), theme from Beetlejuice (Day-O) and Puff the Magic Dragon. Each song includes an accompaniment part for teacher or adult so that the kids can experience the joy of four-hand playing as well! Plus performance tips.
_____ 02505507 TV Themes & Movie Songs............................. $9.95
_____ 02500304 More TV Themes & Movie Songs $9.95

BEST OF JOHN MAYER FOR EASY PIANO
15 of Mayer's best arranged for easy piano, including: Daughters • Gravity • My Stupid Mouth • No Such Thing • Waiting on the World to Change • Who Says • Why Georgia • Your Body Is a Wonderland • and more.
_____ 02501705 Easy Piano $16.99

POKEMON 2 B.A. MASTER
This great songbook features easy piano arrangements of 13 tunes from the hit TV series: 2.B.A. Master • Double Trouble (Team Rocket) • Everything Changes • Misty's Song • My Best Friends • Pokémon (Dance Mix) • Pokémon Theme • PokéRAP • The Time Has Come (Pikachu's Goodbye) • Together, Forever • Viridian City • What Kind of Pokémon Are You? • You Can Do It (If You Really Try). Includes a full-color, 8-page pull-out section featuring characters and scenes from this super hot show.
_____ 02500145 Easy Piano $12.95

POPULAR CHRISTMAS CAROLS COLORING BOOK
Kids are sure to love this fun holiday songbook! It features five-finger piano arrangements of seven Christmas classics, complete with coloring pages throughout! Songs include: Deck the Hall • Good King Wenceslas • Jingle Bells • Jolly Old St. Nicholas • O Christmas Tree • Up on the Housetop • We Wish You a Merry Christmas.
_____ 02500276 Five-Finger Piano............................... $6.95

PUFF THE MAGIC DRAGON & 54 OTHER ALL-TIME CHILDREN'S FAVORITESONGS
55 timeless songs enjoyed by generations of kids, and sure to be favorites for years to come. Songs include: A-Tisket A-Tasket • Alouette • Eensy Weensy Spider • The Farmer in the Dell • I've Been Working on the Railroad • If You're Happy and You Know It • Joy to the World • Michael Finnegan • Oh Where, Oh Where Has My Little Dog Gone • Silent Night • Skip to My Lou • This Old Man • and many more.
_____ 02500017 Big-Note Piano............................... $12.95

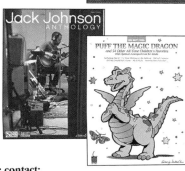

More Great Piano/Vocal Books

FROM CHERRY LANE

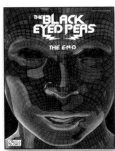
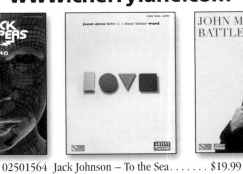

For a complete listing of Cherry Lane titles available, including contents listings, please visit our web site at

www.cherrylane.com

02501590	Sara Bareilles – Kaleidoscope Heart	$17.99
02501136	Sara Bareilles – Little Voice	$16.95
00102353	Sara Bareilles – Once Upon Another Time	$12.99
02501505	The Black Eyed Peas – The E.N.D.	$19.99
02502171	The Best of Boston	$17.95
02501614	Zac Brown Band – The Foundation	$19.99
02501618	Zac Brown Band – You Get What You Give	$19.99
02501123	Buffy the Vampire Slayer – Once More with Feeling	$18.95
02500665	Sammy Cahn Songbook	$24.95
02501688	Colbie Caillat – All of You	$17.99
02501454	Colbie Caillat – Breakthrough	$17.99
02501127	Colbie Caillat – Coco	$16.95
02500838	Best of Joe Cocker	$16.95
02502165	John Denver Anthology – Revised	$22.95
02500002	John Denver Christmas	$14.95
02502166	John Denver's Greatest Hits	$17.95
02502151	John Denver – A Legacy in Song (Softcover)	$24.95
02500566	Poems, Prayers and Promises: The Art and Soul of John Denver	$19.95
02500326	John Denver – The Wildlife Concert	$17.95
02500501	John Denver and the Muppets: A Christmas Together	$9.95
02501186	The Dresden Dolls – The Virginia Companion	$39.95
02509922	The Songs of Bob Dylan	$29.95
02500497	Linda Eder – Gold	$14.95
02500396	Linda Eder – Christmas Stays the Same	$17.95
02502209	Linda Eder – It's Time	$17.95
02501542	Foreigner – The Collection	$19.99
02500535	Erroll Garner Anthology	$19.95
02500318	Gladiator	$12.95
02502126	Best of Guns N' Roses	$17.95
02502072	Guns N' Roses – Selections from Use Your Illusion I and II	$17.95
02500014	Sir Roland Hanna Collection	$19.95
02501447	Eric Hutchinson – Sounds Like This	$17.99
02500856	Jack Johnson – Anthology	$19.99
02501140	Jack Johnson – Sleep Through the Static	$16.95
02501564	Jack Johnson – To the Sea	$19.99
02501546	Jack's Mannequin – *The Glass Passenger* and *The Dear Jack EP*	$19.99
02500834	The Best of Rickie Lee Jones	$16.95
02500381	Lenny Kravitz – Greatest Hits	$14.95
02501318	John Legend – Evolver	$19.99
02500822	John Legend – Get Lifted	$16.99
02503701	Man of La Mancha	$11.95
02501047	Dave Matthews Band – Anthology	$24.95
02502192	Dave Matthews Band – Under the Table and Dreaming	$17.95
02501514	John Mayer Anthology – Volume 1	$22.99
02501504	John Mayer – Battle Studies	$19.99
02500987	John Mayer – Continuum	$16.95
02500681	John Mayer – Heavier Things	$16.95
02500563	John Mayer – Room for Squares	$16.95
02500081	Natalie Merchant – Ophelia	$14.95
02502446	Jason Mraz – Love Is a Four Letter Word	$19.99
02500863	Jason Mraz – Mr. A-Z	$17.95
02501467	Jason Mraz – We Sing. We Dance. We Steal Things.	$19.99
02502895	Nine	$17.95
02501411	Nine – Film Selections	$19.99
02500425	Time and Love: The Art and Soul of Laura Nyro	$21.99
02502204	The Best of Metallica	$17.95
02501497	Ingrid Michaelson – Everybody	$17.99
02501496	Ingrid Michaelson – Girls and Boys	$19.99
02501768	Ingrid Michaelson – Human Again	$17.99
02501529	Monte Montgomery Collection	$24.99
02500857	Anna Nalick – Wreck of the Day	$16.95
02501336	Amanda Palmer – Who Killed Amanda Palmer?	$17.99
02501004	Best of Gram Parsons	$16.95
02500010	Tom Paxton – The Honor of Your Company	$17.95
02507962	Peter, Paul & Mary – Holiday Concert	$17.95
02500145	Pokemon 2.B.A. Master	$12.95
02500026	The Prince of Egypt	$16.95
02500660	Best of Bonnie Raitt	$17.95
02502189	The Bonnie Raitt Collection	$22.95
02502088	Bonnie Raitt – Luck of the Draw	$14.95
02507958	Bonnie Raitt – Nick of Time	$14.95
02502218	Kenny Rogers – The Gift	$16.95
02501577	She & Him – Volume One	$16.99
02501578	She & Him – Volume Two	$16.99
02500414	Shrek	$16.99
02500536	Spirit – Stallion of the Cimarron	$16.95
02500166	Steely Dan – Anthology	$17.95
02500622	Steely Dan – Everything Must Go	$14.95
02500284	Steely Dan – Two Against Nature	$14.95
02500344	Billy Strayhorn: An American Master	$17.95
02500515	Barbra Streisand – Christmas Memories	$16.95
02502164	Barbra Streisand – The Concert	$22.95
02500550	Essential Barbra Streisand	$24.95
02502228	Barbra Streisand – Higher Ground	$17.99
02501065	Barbra Streisand – Live in Concert 2006	$19.95
02501485	Barbra Streisand – Love Is the Answer	$19.99
02501722	Barbra Streisand – What Matters Most	$19.99
02502178	The John Tesh Collection	$17.95
02503623	John Tesh – A Family Christmas	$15.95
02503630	John Tesh – Grand Passion	$16.95
02500307	John Tesh – Pure Movies 2	$16.95
02501068	The Evolution of Robin Thicke	$19.95
02500565	Thoroughly Modern Millie	$17.99
02501399	Best of Toto	$19.99
02502175	Tower of Power – Silver Anniversary	$17.95
02501403	Keith Urban – Defying Gravity	$17.99
02501008	Keith Urban – Love, Pain & The Whole Crazy Thing	$17.95
02501141	Keith Urban – Greatest Hits	$16.99
02502198	The "Weird Al" Yankovic Anthology	$17.95
02500334	Maury Yeston – December Songs	$17.95
02502225	The Maury Yeston Songbook	$19.95

See your local music dealer or contact:

cherry lane
music company

EXCLUSIVELY DISTRIBUTED BY

HAL•LEONARD CORPORATION

7777 W. BLUEMOUND RD. P.O. BOX 13819 MILWAUKEE, WI 53213

Prices, contents and availability subject to change without notice.

1112